ANIMAL EARS

VrAW BL VWM

David M. Schwartz *is an award-winning author of children's books, on a wide variety of topics, loved by children around the world.* Dwight Kuhn's *scientific expertise and artful eye work together with the camera to capture the awesome wonder of the natural world.*

For a free color catalog describing Gareth Stevens Publishing's list of high-quality books and multimedia programs, call 1-800-542-2595 (USA) or 1-800-461-9120 (Canada). Gareth Stevens Publishing's Fax: (414) 225-0377.

Library of Congress Cataloging-in-Publication Data

Schwartz, David M.
    Animal ears / by David M. Schwartz; photographs by Dwight Kuhn.
       p. cm. — (Look once, look again)
    Includes bibliographical references and index.
    Summary: Introduces the unique ears of bats, mosquitoes, owls, frogs, grasshoppers, shrews, and rabbits.
    ISBN 0-8368-2576-4 (lib. bdg.)
    1. Ear—Juvenile literature. [1. Ear. 2. Hearing. 3. Senses and sensation. 4. Animals—Physiology.] I. Kuhn, Dwight, ill. II. Title. III. Series: Schwartz, David M. Look once, look again.
QL948.S43 2000
573.8'9—dc21   99-048372

This North American edition first published in 2000 by
Gareth Stevens Publishing
1555 North RiverCenter Drive, Suite 201
Milwaukee, Wisconsin 53212 USA

First published in the United States in 1998 by Creative Teaching Press, Inc., P. O. Box 6017, Cypress, California, 90630-0017.

Text © 1998 by David M. Schwartz; photographs © 1998 by Dwight Kuhn. Additional end matter © 2000 by Gareth Stevens, Inc.

Printed in the United States of America

1 2 3 4 5 6 7 8 9 04 03 02 01 00

ANIMAL EARS

by David M. Schwartz
photographs by Dwight Kuhn

A SPRINGBOARDS INTO
SCIENCE
SERIES

Gareth Stevens Publishing
MILWAUKEE

This ear belongs to a mammal that flies at night. It helps the animal navigate in the dark.

This big brown bat catches hundreds of insects every night using echoes.

When a bat flies, it makes clicking sounds. The clicks bounce off objects. The bat hears the echoes and can tell where the objects are located.

Does this look like a bottlebrush? Actually, it is the feathery antenna of an insect that buzzes.

Everyone knows the buzz of a mosquito. A mosquito hears with its bushy antennae. They are its ears. When a male hears a female, he flies to her so they can mate.

8

Some people call this an ear, but it does not hear.
Yet, this bird can hear mice a half mile (3/4 kilometer) away.

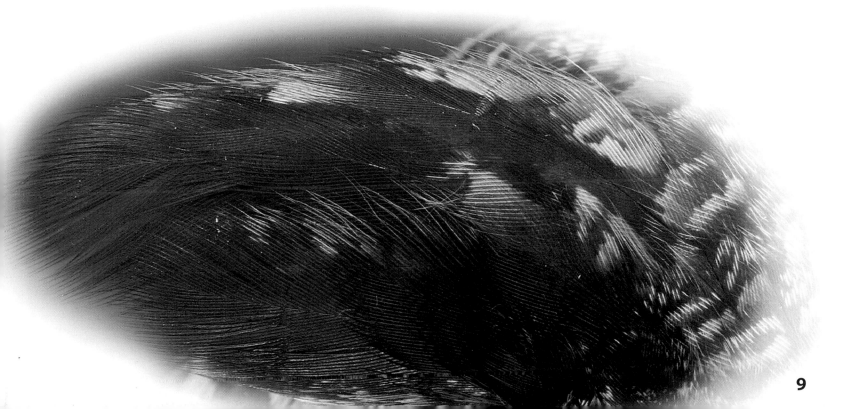

A great horned owl has two ear tufts. Ear tufts are long feathers on top of an owl's head. They are not ears. An owl's true ears are on the sides of its head hidden under feathers.

10

This ear looks like a rusty penny. The animal it belongs to hears croaking sounds in a pond.

A frog's eardrum is on the outside of its head. A frog can hear above or under water. During mating season, females listen for the croaking sounds of the males.

This ear belongs
to one of the
smallest mammals.

A shrew's ear is hidden under its fur. Some scientists think shrews make clicking sounds and listen for echoes in the same way bats do.

When these big ears hear danger, this animal hops to safety.

Big ears help rabbits hear and cool off. Rabbits can turn both ears together or one at a time.

This white sac is the ear of an insect that hops and eats grass.

Most insects do not hear, but grasshoppers do. This grasshopper's ear sacs sit on its hind legs.

Some grasshoppers sing by rubbing their back legs on their front wings. Each kind of grasshopper makes a different sound.

A.

B.

C.

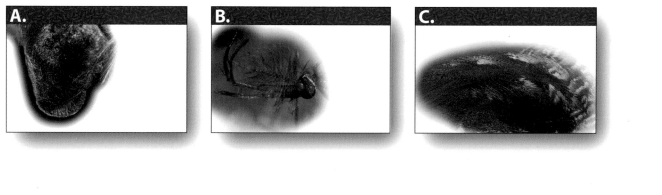

D.

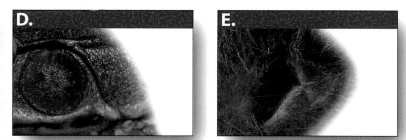

E.

F.

G.

Look closely. Do you know to which animals these ears belong?

19

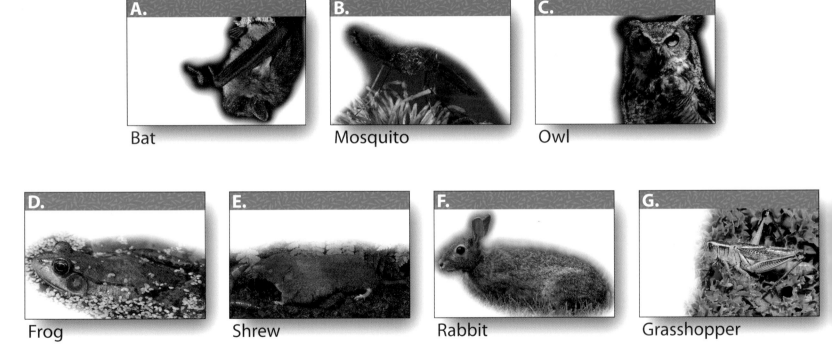

A.

Bat

B.

Mosquito

C.

Owl

D.

Frog

E.

Shrew

F.

Rabbit

G.

Grasshopper

How many were you able to identify correctly?

antennae: the "feelers" on the top of an insect's head.

bat: a night-flying mammal that navigates with echoes.

clicks: slight, sharp noises or sounds.

eardrum: a thin membrane inside the ear that vibrates when sound waves strike it.

echoes: repeated sounds caused by the reflection of sound waves.

frog: an amphibian with long hind legs and webbed feet. Amphibians live both on land and in the water.

insects: small animals with three pairs of legs, one or two sets of wings, a head, a thorax, and an abdomen.

mammal: an animal that nourishes its young with milk from the mother.

mate _(v)_: to join together for the purpose of creating offspring.

mosquito: a small, two-winged insect. The female has long mouthparts with which she punctures other animals to drink their blood.

navigate: find a way through a course.

owl: a nocturnal bird of prey with large eyes, a hooked beak, and talons.

sac: a pouch on an animal or plant.

shrew: a small, nocturnal animal with a pointed snout, small eyes, and soft fur.

tufts: clusters of items, such as feathers.

ACTIVITIES

What Do You Hear?

Close your eyes, and pretend you're on an African safari. What do you hear? What kind of sounds do the gorillas and lions make? Now close your eyes, and pretend you're floating down the Amazon River in South America. What do you hear? Close your eyes, and pretend you're in the middle of New York City. What do you hear now?

Check Out Those Ears!

Get ready for a fun day at the zoo by first doing some research at the library or on the Internet. Find photographs of all the animals that you expect to see at the zoo. Point out their ears. What size and shape are they? Can you always see the ears, or are some ears hidden? Do all of the animals have ears, or do they have some other way of sensing sounds?

What Was That?

Some of the sounds you hear every day are easy to recognize. Honking horns, barking dogs, racing engines of cars and trucks — you could probably recognize them with your eyes closed. Play a game with your friends. Have each person take a turn wearing a blindfold, while the rest of the group makes different sounds. To start, try bouncing a ball, tearing a piece of paper, or hammering a nail. Can you guess what all of the sounds are?

Quiet, Please.

Go to a park or another natural area, and look and listen. Take a notebook with you to record all you observe and hear. Do you think you would enjoy growing up to be a naturalist, studying wild animals and plants? Do some research to find out how to become one.

More Books to Read

Animal Senses. Animal Survival (series). Michel Barré (Gareth Stevens)

Animals Are Not Like Us (series). Graham Meadows (Gareth Stevens)

Bat Magic for Kids. Animal Magic for Kids (series). Kathryn T. Lundberg (Gareth Stevens)

Hearing. Exploring Our Senses (series). Henry Pluckrose (Gareth Stevens)

Insects. Wonderful World of Animals (series). Beatrice MacLeod (Gareth Stevens)

Nightprowlers: Everyday Creatures Under Every Night Sky. Jerry Emory (Harcourt)

Sound. Science Works! (series). Steve Parker (Gareth Stevens)

Videos

Animal Senses. (DK Publishing)

Animals Hear in Many Ways. (Phoenix/BFA)

Sound Sense. (Coronet)

Web Sites

www.thewildones.org/Animals/echolocation.html

168.99.7.17/fletcht/Hearing.html

Some web sites stay current longer than others. For further web sites, use your search engines to locate the following topics: *bats, eardrums, ears, echolocation, grasshoppers,* and *hearing.*

INDEX